CAPE COD LIGHT
The Lighthouse at Dangerfield

To Fran

ISBN 0-9653283-3-3

10 9 8 7 6 5 4 3 2

This book is adapted from the 1969 book by Paul Giambarba entitled *The Lighthouse at Dangerfield*, published by Little Brown and Company in association with the Atlantic Monthly Press.

Additional copies may be obtained by contacting:
On Cape Publications
P.O. Box 218
Yarmouth Port, MA 02675
email: oncapepubs@yahoo.com
Toll Free: 1-877-662-5839

Printed in Korea

CAPE COD LIGHT
The Lighthouse at Dangerfield

Written & Illustrated by Paul Giambarba

On
Cape Publications

Yarmouth Port, Massachusetts

Dangerfield is what the Pilgrims
called Truro, on Cape Cod.
It's a good name for this narrow land
off the Massachusetts coast
that sticks out into the stormy Atlantic Ocean.

Miles and miles of sandbars lie along the outer shore and reach out into the sea. They are hidden by shallow water. They have caused hundreds of vessels of all kinds and sizes to be wrecked on them.

To warn ships away from such disaster, Cape Cod Light or Highland Light, as it is known on the Cape, was built more than two hundred years ago in 1797, when George Washington was the President of the United States.

Sailors could see
Highland Light
and steer away
from the danger.

The first tower stood
at the top of the cliff,
near its edge.

Over the years waves beat against the cliff and washed more and more of it into the sea. Soon the old lighthouse was in danger of being washed away.

But before that happened,
a new tower was built back
from the cliff's edge.

Beside it a house was built
for the lighthouse keeper
and his family.

When a heavy gale or hurricane blew, the house would rattle and shake. The keeper and his family sometimes left their cozy home for safety in the brick tower.

Sometimes they had to
shout to be heard over
the roar of the surf
and the howling wind.

Every day at sunset
the keeper entered the tower.

It was his duty to make
certain that the light shone
every night for all to see.

He climbed the sixty-nine steps to the top of the lighthouse. With a small lamp he lighted the wicks of the kerosene lamps in the lantern room.

Then he climbed down the
ladder to the deck below.

There he "wound the clock."
This was a machine of weights
and gears that turned
the great glass lenses
around the lamps.

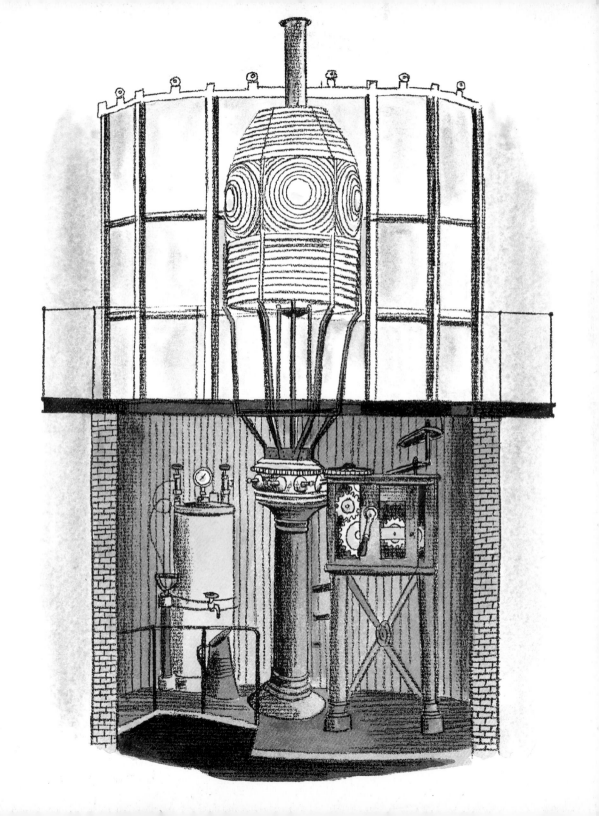

The light of the lamps shone through the great glass lenses. The lenses worked like big magnifying glasses.

The light blinked as the lenses moved slowly around it.

The lenses made the light so strong
that it could be seen twenty miles away.

The children learned how to sleep with the great light shining as bright as the sun through their bedroom curtains.

At daybreak the keeper snuffed out the lamps and
filled them with oil again for the night to come.

Smoke from the lamps
left soot on the lenses,
which the keeper had
to clean off so the light
would stay bright.

His family helped shine
the brass and wash
the windows of the
lantern, too.

This was just one of many chores that kept a lighthouse keeper's family busy. Everybody pitched in to get the jobs done. The children also went to school every day and had homework to do as well.

Once a year the keeper had to whitewash the tower and paint the ironwork of the lantern. He did this in late May before the flies began buzzing.

He was hoisted up
in a basket almost one
hundred feet in the air
to paint the lightning
rod and the cap of
the lantern.

On hot summer nights the glass sides of the lantern were covered with moths attracted to the light.

In very foggy
weather sailors could not
see the light at all.

The keeper made the
loud foghorn blow to
warn them away from
the dangerous sandbars.

Stormy days were the worst of all. No matter how bad the storm, the light must not fail. The keeper stayed in the tower and kept a lookout for ships in trouble.

On the twentieth of April in 1852 the keeper saw the English vessel *Josepha* strike the bars and break up.

The keeper and the minister of Dangerfield hurried to the beach, and there they found two sailors, the only men aboard who had reached shore alive. Both were taken to the keeper's house and cared for.

One of the sailors later became captain of an Atlantic packet,
a vessel that made regular trips across the ocean to Europe.
Whenever he passed the Cape Cod Light he dipped the
ship's flag in thanks to the light and its keeper.

In 1996 the tower and buildings were moved back again from the eroding cliff. The large stone in the foreground is where the lighthouse had been. Today everything looks like this, and people come from all over the world to visit Cape Cod Light. It still shines as it always has since George Washington was President of the United States.